Presented to:

Never Forget The Difference You've Made

Made in United States
North Haven, CT
06 December 2022

28087375R10065